**Crafty
Inventions**

suoitnevnI
ytfarC

**Crafty
Inventions**

**Crafty
Inventions**

suoitnevnI
ytfarC

Crafty Inventions

Crafty Inventions

Crafty Inventions

Crafty Inventions

Crafty Inventions

Crafty Inventions

UNDERWATER
MACHINES

by Gerry Bailey

illustrated by Steve Boulter
and Jan Smith

Reading Adviser:
Susan Kesselring, M.A., Literacy Educator
Rosemount-Apple Valley-Eagan
(Minnesota) School District

PiCTURE WiNDOW BOOKS
www.picturewindowbooks.com

First American edition published in 2005 by

Picture Window Books
5115 Excelsior Boulevard
Suite 232
Minneapolis, MN 55416
877-845-8392
www.picturewindowbooks.com

Publisher: Felicia Law

Design director: Tracy Carrington

Project manager: Karen Foster

Author: Gerry Bailey

Editors: Rosalind Beckman, Christianne Jones,
Jackie Wolfe

Designed by: Jacqueline Palmer; assisted by Simon
Brewster, Will Webster, Tracy Davies

Cartoon illustrations: Steve Boulter (Advocate)

Make-and-do: Jan Smith

Model-maker: Tim Draper

Photo studio: Steve Lumb

Photo research: Diana Morris

Scanning: Imagewrite

Digital workflow: Edward MacDermott

Library of Congress Cataloging-in-Publication Data
Bailey, Gerry.
Underwater machines / written by Gerry Bailey ;
illustrated by Steve Boulter and Jan Smith.— 1st
American ed.
p. cm. — (Crafty inventions)
Originally published: London : Allegra Pub., 2003.
Includes index.
ISBN 1-4048-1045-5
1. Underwater exploration—Juvenile literature.
2. Submersibles—Juvenile literature. I. Boulter, Steve, ill.
II. Smith, Jan, 1956- ill. III. Title.

GC65.B24 2005
551.46—dc22   2004028641

Photo Credits
Art Directors and Trip: 6b, 18b, 29tr.;
Bettmann/Corbis: 41tr.; Ecoscene: 9t.;
Steve Kaufman/Corbis: 35b.; Courtesy of the
Institute for Exploration, Mystic, Connecticut:
38b.; IWM/TRH Pictures: 25tr.; PA/Topham:
5tr.; Photri/Topham: 30b, 42b.;Picturepoint/
Topham: 10b, 13tr, 17t, 21t, 26b.; Bruce
Robison/Corbis: 14bl.; Jeffrey L. Rotman/
Corbis: 22b.; TRH Pictures: 33tr.; UPPA/
Topham: 37tr.

Crafty Inventions

UNDERWATER MACHINES

Table of Contents

Can We Breathe Under the Sea?

Most of the Earth's surface is covered with water, so there is much to explore and discover. But humans are not equipped to breathe under water. This means that to explore the oceans, humans will either have to grow gills—or take some air with them.

Since earliest times, people have learned how to dive under water for long periods of time. They do this by holding their breath for as long as possible.

Ancient Greek and Roman divers hunted under water for pearls, sponges, and shells as long ago as 4500 B.C.

Divers in the Persian Gulf were the first to use goggles. They were made of polished, clear tortoiseshell. But these divers were still limited by how long they could hold their breath, and how deep they could dive safely.

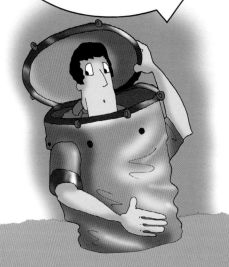

I want to stay under water for much longer than just a couple of minutes.

WHAT COULD THEY DO?

- Divers could try to hold their breath for even longer, but they'd still run out of oxygen after a short while.

- Somehow, divers had to carry the air they needed into the water with them. Or perhaps it could be sent down to them in some way.

- In 1715, an English diver named John Lethbridge had an idea. He made a special suit out of wood and leather.

- Then, in 1837, a German engineer named Augustus Seibe came up with an improved diving suit. It included waterproof clothing and a helmet.

I'll make a waterproof diving suit that can be supplied with air from the surface. A pump on board a boat will force air down a tube and into the diver's helmet. Divers will be able to stay under water long enough to work or explore.

Diving suits made the exploration of wrecks as well as underwater terrain possible.

Watertight

A **diving suit** consists of a waterproof suit and helmet that is supplied with air from the surface. The diver receives air or breathing gas through a hose connected to a special pump on a boat directly above. The first diving helmets were made of copper, and the suit was of canvas. Today, helmets are usually made of lighter material such as **fiberglass**. Special diving masks also can be used with these helmets. In addition to the air hose, other hoses may be used to deliver hot water to the suit to keep the diver warm, or high pressure air to operate machinery. Electricity to operate power tools can be supplied by wires, while gases for welding torches are supplied by hose.

Safe diving

Water creates pressure on things just as air does. But water pressure is greater. The pressure on a diver 33 feet (10 meters) below the surface is twice as great as the air pressure at the surface. At 66 feet (20 m), the pressure is three times greater, and so on.

Water pressure makes diving dangerous, so divers must take special care. Without a diving suit, the pressure in a diver's lungs does not equal the water pressure outside them. If the pressure is too great, an injury called barotrauma, or squeeze, may result. So divers must descend very slowly and carefully. Where the ocean is very deep, the pressure becomes great enough to crush even a submarine. Any diving suit or vehicle at these levels must be pressurized. Modern diving suits are pressurized, just like submarines and other deep-sea vehicles, to equal the force of the water outside.

A modern diving suit is pressurized to allow the diver to work at great depths.

AROUND THE BENDS

Early divers dreaded getting the bends when they swam upward from the seabed. A diver who breathes compressed air absorbs large amounts of nitrogen into the blood. The nitrogen is breathed out as the diver ascends. But if the diver comes up too fast, bubbles of nitrogen gas form in the blood. They can block the flow of blood and kill the diver. The bends can be avoided if the diver rises slowly.

Inventor's words

barotrauma
bends
diving suit
fiberglass
submarine
water pressure

Make a set of picture portholes

You will need

cardboard • tissue paper
shells • pebbles
metallic cardboard
colored paper
sucker sticks • netting
double-sided tape
craft glue
glitter glue • scissors
paints and brush

1 Cut out two flat circles of cardboard. Use tissue paper, paint, and glue to make a seascape on one of them.

2 Glue on shells and small pebbles to make the seabed.

3 Using metallic cardboard and sucker sticks, make an Atlantis lost city design or a sunken treasure ship. Add netting and tissue paper to make weeds, and glue on colored fish shapes.

4 Cut a long strip of cardboard, and, using double-sided tape, stick this along the edge to enclose the cardboard circle.

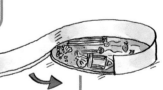

5 Cut out the center of the other circle to make a ring. Tape and glue this to the top of the porthole. Decorate with paint and glitter glue.

How Can I Dive Safely by Myself?

Diving suits and submersible vehicles certainly allow people to explore under water or to carry out tasks such as salvage work. But they don't allow divers much freedom to move. Wouldn't it be great if they could swim around like fish? But how would divers breathe?

People have practiced breath-hold diving for thousands of years. But without special breathing equipment, each dive is short and frantic.

Divers used snorkels made of hollow reed around 100 A.D. With diving bells and diving suits, people could stay under water for longer, but they relied on others for air.

Methods of underwater exploration were improved during the 19th century. However, an individual breathing device was still needed to supply and regulate air to a diver below the surface.

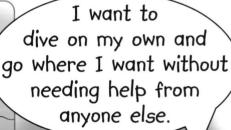

> I want to dive on my own and go where I want without needing help from anyone else.

WHAT HAPPENED NEXT?

- In the 1940s, two Frenchmen—Jacques-Yves Cousteau, a naval officer, and Emile Gagnan, an engineer—began working on an artificial lung.

- They believed that a container of breathable gas could be carried with the diver under the water.

- A tank that could be carried on the diver's back and filled with compressed air seemed to be the answer.

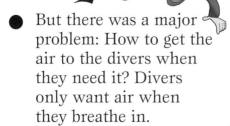

- But there was a major problem: How to get the air to the divers when they need it? Divers only want air when they breathe in.

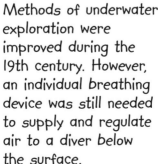

I'll solve the problem with a special valve called a demand valve. A tube will run from the tank to the valve, which the diver holds in his or her mouth. The valve will supply air only when the diver breathes in.

An aqualung is part of a diver's equipment and ensures the ability to breathe easily.

Tanked up

An aqualung is an artificial lung that allows divers to breathe by themselves under water. It is made up of a light-weight aluminum tank, a tube running from the tank to a special valve, and a harness for strapping the tank onto a diver's back. The tank carries a supply of compressed air that can be filled to a pressure of 3,000 pounds (1,361 kilograms) per square inch.

The special valve is called a demand valve, or demand regulator, and is held in the diver's mouth. When the diver breathes in, the valve supplies air. When the diver breathes out, the valve pushes air out into the seawater. A diver with one tank can stay at a depth of 40 feet (12.2 m) for one hour. Today, most divers carry two tanks rather than one.

Scuba diving

There are two main kinds of diving. Breath-hold diving requires no equipment except, perhaps, for a snorkel, fins, and a mask. Scuba **diving uses tanks to supply air to a diver.** *Scuba* **stands for self-contained underwater breathing apparatus.**

Air is supplied to scuba divers from one or more tanks strapped to their backs. The amount of air used up by divers will depend on how strenuous their activity is or how deep they dive. A regulator controls the flow of air so that the pressure inside the diver's lungs is the same as the pressure of the water outside. If it isn't, a diver can be badly hurt. Scuba divers may also wear a wet suit to stay warm and a weighted belt to keep them at a certain depth. They may also carry a buoyancy compensator that can be inflated to help maintain a required depth. Fins and a mask are also used.

UNDERWATER GIZMOS

Divers today often carry complex equipment under water. Special cameras and lights are used for underwater photographs, film, and even videos. Electronic equipment is used to communicate with the surface or other divers to help their search for sunken ships, and mini-computers can be worn on the wrist.

Scuba divers working on an oil rig in the Atlantic Ocean

Inventor's words

aqualung
buoyancy
compensator
compressed
demand valve
scuba • wet suit

Make a deep-sea diver

1 Out of the clay, sculpt a diver's head inside a deep-sea helmet, two arms, and two legs.

2 Make a square body unit out of two small boxes glued together. Decorate with corrugated metallic cardboard or something similar.

3 Cover the clay limbs in craft glue and layers of crepe paper to look like a textured diving suit. Coil string around the arms and legs at intervals for extra effect.

4 Glue a piece of acetate over the front of the diver's mask to look like glass. Glue a bottle cap to the top of the helmet, and attach a piece of string for a lifeline.

5 Then glue the diver together, painting on gloves and boots.

Can I Stay Longer Under Water?

Ever since humans started diving for pearls or sponges, they have looked for ways to stay under water for longer periods of time. The first device to allow divers to breathe under water was the diving bell. The problem was people could only dive to a depth of about 66 feet (20 m).

The first diving bells were open to the water at the bottom. The air pressure that existed in the diving bell kept the water from getting inside.

Extra air was provided by a hose that connected the diving bell to the surface. Often, these devices could accommodate more than one diver.

A really useful wooden diving bell was invented by Guglielmo de Loreno in 1535. But it couldn't be used in very deep water. By the 19th century, scientists wanted to study undersea life and needed something better.

If only we could find a way of exploring the seabed!

WHAT DID THEY DO?

- Clearly, a device that was open to the water at the bottom would not work for long. What was needed was an enclosed capsule.

- But a capsule shaped like a diving bell with a solid floor wasn't the answer. Water pressure would be very high, and the bell design wouldn't take the pressure evenly.

- A sphere would be better. Inside, explorers could sit on a flat surface or on seats.

- Wood would be useless because the pressure of the sea at great depths would crush it. By 1930, an American named Otis Barton had the solution.

I'll construct a spherical steel container called a bathysphere. It will have portholes made of thick glass. The bathysphere can be suspended underneath a ship, then lowered to a depth of about 2,970 feet (905 m).

Barton's bathysphere allowed naturalist William Beebe to study marine life close-up.

Hanging on

A **bathysphere** is a spherical container that can be hung underneath a ship. It is able to maintain ground-level air pressure inside, so it can be lowered to great depths below the surface of the sea without harming its occupants. The bathysphere had small round windows called **ports,** so divers could look out. It was attached to a mother ship and had no means of **propulsion** of its own. Otis Barton designed the first bathysphere, and in 1930, he and the naturalist William Beebe made the first dive in it. They descended into waters off the island of Bermuda, where Beebe was able to study plant and animal life at depths never reached before.

Deep-sea fish

The deepest parts of the oceans are pitch black, and the huge pressure from the surrounding water would crush any land-living animal. However, the animals that live there adapt to these difficult conditions.

These include extraordinary deep-sea fish that have special features to help them survive. All have bodies that can withstand the crushing water pressure. Many, such as the angler fish and gulper eel, have huge mouths filled with long, needle-sharp teeth. This is because food is scarce on the ocean floor, and a huge mouth is less likely to miss what is available. Some deep-sea fish are able to make their own light, which is produced by organs called photophores inside the fish's body. The dragonfish, for instance, has rows of lights along its side. The angler fish has a light dangling from a fin, or barbel, in front of its huge mouth to lure smaller fish in.

BIG MOUTH!

Many deep-sea fish have specially modified mouths, or jaws. The slackjaw, for instance, has no floor to its mouth. The viperfish has an extra joint in the head, which increases its bite. As the jaws open, its heart and gills are pushed back to make way for the food. The fangs of some viperfish are so long, they stick out of the fish's mouth even when its mouth is closed.

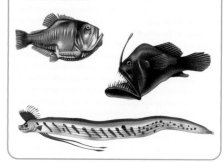

Early naturalists were surprised to find fish living so deep in the oceans.

Inventor's words

barbel
bathysphere
deep-sea fish
port
photophore
propulsion

Make a lantern fish

You will need

balloon • newspaper
tissue paper
foil and metallic cardboard
thick cardboard
styrofoam cup
flexible wire
craft knife • scissors
craft glue • marbles
paints and brush
glow paint stick

1 To make the fish, cover the balloon in strips of newspaper soaked in craft glue mixed with water. When dry, cut a semi-circular mouth shape into the body, and pull down the flap.

2 Cut out some triangular teeth from thick cardboard. Glue them in place around the edges of the mouth.

3 Glue the styrofoam cup over the tail-end of the fish. Cut a slot into the base of the cup, then cut a tail fin from cardboard to slot in. Glue to attach.

4 Make eyestalks from two small, rolled up pieces of cardboard. Wedge a marble eye onto each and then glue them onto the fish. Cut out two fins from metallic cardboard and attach to the body.

5 Decorate the fish with tissue paper scales, then bend a piece of wire to make the "lantern," attaching a crumpled foil lure to the end of it. Attach the wire to the forehead, and glue to reinforce.

15

Can Boats Travel Under the Sea?

Boats and ships have always sailed across the oceans on the surface of the water. No one thought seriously about taking a boat under water, as it would be difficult to power. But that didn't stop some inventive people from thinking of ways to build a submarine.

The first underwater craft was simply a rowing boat covered with waterproof hides. It was demonstrated in 1620 by Dutch scientist Cornelius van Drebel.

Then, in 1776, during the American Revolution, a student named David Bushnell designed a one-man attack submarine called the American Turtle.

A submarine is such a great idea, we've got to find a way to get the navy onboard!

Another American, Robert Fulton, built a copper-covered submarine called the Nautilus in 1801. It was 21 feet (6.4 m) long and could sink ships. But no government showed any interest. Obviously, a better design was needed.

WHAT HAPPENED NEXT?

- Clearly, the development of submarines was based on their abilities as warships.

- While they had to stay under water unseen, they also needed the capability to shoot at and sink surface warships.

- The invention of the gasoline engine and electric batteries made powering a submarine much easier. In 1889, John P. Holland launched a 53-foot (16-m) submarine powered by gasoline and electricity.

- The next challenge was how to find the enemy when the submarine was submerged. Simon Lake came up with the answer in 1902.

A submarine must be able to see above the surface while it is still under water. So, I'll use magnifying lenses and a tube that can be pushed up from the submarine's turret. My periscope will allow the submerged sub to see distant targets.

German-built *Unterseeboote*, or U-boats, were the first really effective submarines. People called them "assassins of the sea."

Staying under

A **submarine** is a ship that can travel under water as well as on the surface. It contains tanks that are filled with water to make it sink and can reach depths of more than 1,450 ft (450 m). Submarines vary in size from about 198 ft (60 m) to more than 495 ft (150 m) in length. The **hull** is usually around 30 ft (9 m) across. About 100-150 crew members work aboard a submarine.

Most submarines are used as warships. On the surface, a submarine operates just like a ship and can cruise at about 20 knots. To dive, the **ballast** tanks are flooded with water, which makes the submarine heavier. **Diving planes**, a type of wing, are tilted to help the craft descend. To resurface, water is blown out of the ballast tanks by **compressed** air, or the diving planes are tilted to angle the submarine up.

Streamlining

Streamlining, or a smooth-flowing shape, is as important to ships and submarines as it is to aircraft. A poorly shaped craft, such as a rectangular barge, disturbs the water as it moves. The disturbance is called turbulence. Streamlining avoids turbulence.

When a streamlined craft such as a submarine moves through the water, it pushes the water aside. The water flows around the shape and comes together again behind it. A streamlined shape is rounded at the front and pointed at the back—just like a submarine. Scientists demonstrate how water flows around different-shaped objects by adding streaks of dye to the water. The dye flows evenly, until it hits the object. The resulting streaks of dye indicate the shape of the currents that flow around an object and the amount of turbulence caused.

You can see that the craft and fish in this picture have a similar streamlined shape.

CUTTING-EDGE KILLER

Sharks have a very streamlined shape. This means that they move smoothly through the water, using up as little energy as possible. A shark's sleek shape hardly disturbs the water, so prey are often caught by surprise. Their shape also means sharks can swim very quickly when they want to—as many divers have found out too late!

Inventor's words

ballast
compressed
diving plane
hull
streamlining
submarine
turbulence

Make a whale mobile

You will need

chicken wire
newspaper
string
craft glue
paints and brush

1 Cut out one large and one smaller rectangle of chicken wire. From these sculpt a large and a small whale shape. Add a pair of wire flippers to each.

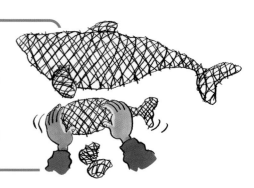

2 Cover the wire with layers of newspaper soaked in craft glue mixed with water.

3 Paint the whales, drawing in the eyes and some barnacles.

4 Make a hole in the top of the larger whale's head. Thread through some string to hang it, and join the two whales together by the same method.

Just How Deep Can I Dive?

When William Beebe accompanied Otis Barton on their historic descent into the Caribbean Sea, he was able to observe sea life down to a depth of 3,046 ft (923 m). But the oceans are much, much deeper than that, and it was not long before explorers wanted to reach even greater depths.

A person in a diving suit can descend just several yards beneath the surface of the ocean before being crushed by the weight of the surrounding water.

The bathysphere was a great idea, but it had to be connected to a boat on the surface. With no power of its own, underwater exploration was limited.

Some scientists wanted to explore as deep as 6.2 miles (10 km) below the surface of the oceans. But you'd need a very long chain to pull you back up. Some other means had to be found.

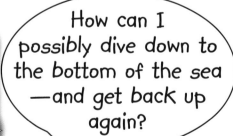

How can I possibly dive down to the bottom of the sea —and get back up again?

WHAT DID THEY DO?

- Swiss scientist Auguste Piccard was interested in exploring the atmosphere around Earth.

- In 1932, he and an assistant ascended 53,463 ft (16,296 m) into the stratosphere in an airtight gondola he had invented that was attached to a balloon.

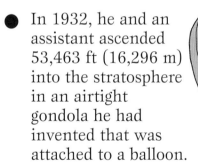

- Piccard now turned to underwater exploration. He realized he could use his skills to build some sort of craft to take him to uncharted depths.

- He came up with an airtight sphere installed under a large boat-shaped hull. But how would he get it to go up as well as down?

Aha! Gasoline and ballast in the hull is the answer. Gasoline is lighter than water, allowing the craft to float. Letting it out and seawater in will cause the bathyscaphe to descend. Letting out the ballast or weights will make it rise again.

Auguste Piccard's bathyscaphe descended to 10.36 feet (3.16 meters) below the Mediterranean Sea in 1953.

A bathyscaphe

A **bathyscaphe** is a manned vehicle used for deep-sea exploration. It consists of a thick-walled steel sphere designed to stand up to the great water pressure at depths. The sphere is attached to a large **hull** that contains several compartments filled with **gasoline**. As gasoline is lighter than water, it gives the bathyscaphe **buoyancy**, or the ability to float.

Battery-driven motors turn screw propellers that move the craft along horizontally. Although the sphere is heavier than water, the hull is lighter than water. To descend, the diver releases some of the gasoline or lets in seawater. The weight of the sphere then pulls the bathyscaphe down. To ascend, the diver releases special weights, called **ballast,** from the hull to lighten it.

Ocean floor

Depth **is the measurement from the surface of the water downward. Scientists use special words to describe the depth of water and the depth of the ocean floor, or seabed, which is the solid base of the ocean.**

But depth can also be measured in terms of the amount of light that penetrates into the water. The photic zone, for example, receives enough light for algae to carry out the process of photosynthesis, or the means of producing food using the energy of sunlight. In the deeper disphotic zone, often called the twilight zone, there is very little light to be seen. In the aphotic zone, there is no light at all.

The ocean floor is home to many unique communities of plants and animals. Can you tell whether the object in this picture is a fish or a clump of seaweed?

TRIESTE IN TRENCH

In 1960, Jacques Piccard and a U.S. Navy lieutenant named Don Walsh made one of the greatest descents into the ocean. They used a bathyscaphe, now called the *Trieste*, to descend 36,003 ft (10,910 m) into the Marianas Trench in the Pacific Ocean. It is the deepest of all ocean trenches— deeper than Mount Everest is high.

Inventor's words

aphotic zone
ballast
bathyscaphe
buoyancy • depth
disphotic zone
gasoline • hull
photic zone
aphotic zone

Make a marine pod

You will need

balloon • newspaper
toilet paper tubes
cardboard • foil
comics and magazines
sucker sticks • bottle caps
empty ribbon or spool tape
drinking straws
pipe cleaners or thin wire
colored electrical wires
glitter glue • scissors
craft glue
paints and brush

1 Cover a balloon with strips of newspaper soaked in craft glue.

2 To make portholes, cut three thin rings from a toilet paper tube. Glue slightly larger cardboard rings to one end of them, and glue a cut-out comic character to the other.

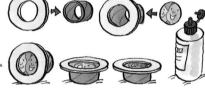

3 Glue the portholes onto the balloon pod, and add bottle caps for decoration. Glue the pod onto an empty spool. Attach sucker stick landing feet. Paint.

4 Make robot arms by threading drinking straws over pipe-cleaners. Thread the center of a pipe cleaner through the top of a bottle cap, and glue it to the sides of the pod. Decorate further with pieces of wire. Repeat for the other arm.

5 Cover three bottle caps in foil to make an array of floodlights. Glue these inside half a painted toilet paper tube, and attach to the pod.

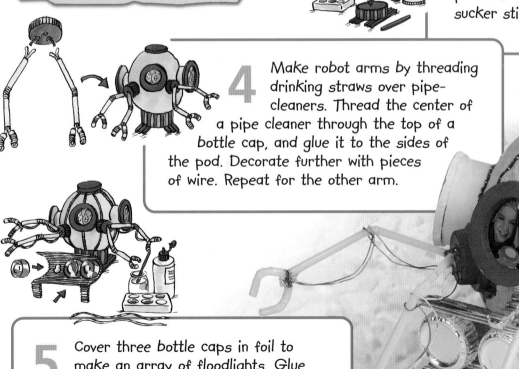

How Can We Sink a Battleship?

The mighty *Tirpitz* was one of the biggest battleships built by Germany during World War II (1939-1945). It was capable of doing great damage to British warships and the convoys that brought food and supplies to Britain from the United States. Somehow, it had to be destroyed.

When the Tirpitz wasn't at sea, it was anchored at a secret base in Norway. From there, it could slip out easily into the North Sea and attack Allied ships.

Its stay in Norway also meant that battleships of the Allied Forces had to patrol the North Sea to keep an eye on it.

While it rested in harbor, the Tirpitz was surrounded by a huge steel net. This prevented torpedoes from blasting her from below. The Germans thought it was completely safe. But was it?

We can't risk the Tirpitz attacking our ships. We must find a way to put it out of action.

WHAT HAPPENED NEXT?

● The *Tirpitz* was attacking ships taking supplies from Britain to Russia. Many Russians were in danger of starvation.

● Air strikes were not effective because the *Tirpitz* was difficult to find in the fjords of Norway, and its guns were powerful.

● A surprise attack was vital. But if it came by sea, enemy ships would be spotted easily.

● Submarines would be better. But a submarine would have difficulty breaking through the strong torpedo nets that protected the *Tirpitz*. The British navy had a brilliant idea.

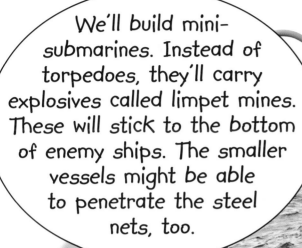

We'll build mini-submarines. Instead of torpedoes, they'll carry explosives called limpet mines. These will stick to the bottom of enemy ships. The smaller vessels might be able to penetrate the steel nets, too.

X-craft were either suspended underneath surface vessels, launched from the deck of larger submarines, or towed to the target area and then released to attack enemy battleships.

Crafty X-craft

X-craft was the name given to the mini-submarines used by the British navy during World War II. Each one carried four men, who lived in a box-like "dry" compartment made of metal. There was no room for cooking facilities, so the crew survived mainly on orange juice and apples. A "wet" compartment allowed a diver to swim from the boat in exercises.

These tiny submarines carried limpet mines, explosive devices that could be planted under an enemy vessel. The diver would swim out of the X-craft to attach the mines, cutting through the anti-torpedo nets that protected battleship moorings. These were perilous missions, where divers would need nerves of steel as they dodged enemy depth charges.

The X-men

Six X-craft set off to destroy the *Tirpitz*. They were towed by a submarine, until they were close to enemy waters. The journey was fraught with danger as they braved the harsh North Sea and German warships, staying under water during the day and surfacing at night. Only two X-craft survived to reach their target.

One X-craft managed to pass through the outer protection before entering a double row of torpedo nets. It stayed just below the surface but then hit some rocks. This caused it to surface with a commotion and become entangled in another net. But it was too close for the *Tirpitz's* big guns to be effective. So, it continued the mission, despite bullets and grenades bouncing off its **hull**. The mines were dropped just before the men abandoned the X-craft and were captured. Another X-craft also dropped its charges before being sunk. But the mines caused so much damage that the *Tirpitz* never went out to sea again.

Built in 1941, the *Tirpitz* was Germany's largest warship. While anchored off Norway, its mission was to attack Arctic convoys and prevent an Allied invasion. It was put out of action in 1944.

OUT OF ACTION

After the 1943 X-craft attack, the *Tirpitz* had to undergo more than 12 months of repairs to make it seaworthy again. But before it could move away, the British Royal Air Force hit it with a Tallboy bomb. The once mighty battleship went up in smoke.

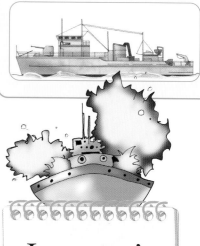

Inventor's words

hull
limpet mine
submarine
X-craft

Build a model warship

You will need

thick cardboard
scissors or craft knife
toothpick
craft glue • pencil
black marker
paints and brush

1 Draw and cut out a series of silhouettes of a warship from thick cardboard. Look at some picture books to get ideas.

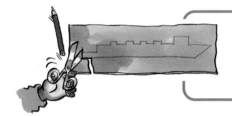

2 Your first shape should be the foreground with little above deck height.

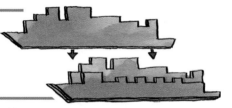

3 The next cutout should have more detail above deck, especially on the upper decks.

4 The third cutout should have the most detail and the highest structures, such as control towers, turrets, and stacks.

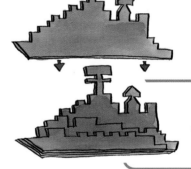

5 Now glue all the silhouettes together for a 3-D warship. Paint and decorate, using toothpicks for guns and mast stalks, and a pen for drawing in the decking and portholes.

What Can Boats Do Under the Sea?

At first, most submarines were used as underwater warships, carrying torpedoes and other weapons. But scientists soon realized they could be used in peacetime for deep-sea exploration. They started to think how submarines could be modified for such work.

A useful submarine, or underwater craft, doesn't have to be large. In fact, the X-craft seemed to be the perfect size for a working mini-submarine.

A craft this size could carry three or four divers. It could stay under water for days instead of hours, giving ample time for observation and exploration.

Even smaller craft that could be lowered from a parent ship would allow a diver to descend as far as 990 ft (300 m) with far less danger involved. But scientists wanted to explore much lower depths.

Let's adapt the submarine idea and use an underwater craft for scientific research.

WHAT HAPPENED NEXT?

- As scientists learned more about the sea and what lay under it, people began to look for new ways to explore it.

- A submersible craft would help divers. It could do some of the divers' jobs and provide more powerful light for them.

- If it were built for strength, it would descend much deeper than a submarine, while keeping its occupants safe.

- Cameras and other equipment connected to the submersible would help map out the seabed and create a geography of the oceans.

We'll build a submersible craft with a very strong hull that can descend to the deep seabed. It'll have windows and will be lowered from a ship, or it'll use its own power to move.

Submersibles use floodlights to light up the ocean floor, where the sunlight doesn't penetrate.

On the ocean floor

A submersible is an underwater craft with a strong hull, so it can descend much deeper than an ordinary submarine. Manned submersibles can descend to around 21,450 ft (6,538 m). The first submersibles were ball-shaped and were lowered by cable from ships. Today, many have motors and propellers, so they can move about the seabed.

Some use electric power supplied by cables from a ship above. All carry their own supply of air, and pressure inside the craft is constant. Most subs have cameras and floodlights, while some have mechanical arms called manipulators that can pick up material from the ocean floor. Many submersibles today are operated by remote control.

The deep sea

Although we know much more about the oceans than ever before, scientists still believe we have explored only about 2 percent of the deep sea.

It was not until the late 19th century that people began to find deep-sea creatures by using dredges. Until then, scientists believed there was no life at the bottom of the oceans. After diving vehicles had improved, more of the oceans and seas were explored. Then, in 1976, biologists first used the epibenthic sled, a kind of scoop. The samples collected from the deep sea contained animals that were previously unknown and gave scientists a better idea of how much life there was on the ocean floor. Submersibles have helped scientists even more; with them, scientists can see the animals and the environment in which they live.

Submersibles are equipped with mechanical arms for collecting animal and plant specimens from the ocean floor.

COLD WATER HOT VENTS

In 1977, oceanographer Robert Ballard and a team of explorers used submersible technology to find amazing hot water vents, or holes, in the floor of the Pacific Ocean. The vents supported a whole life system, including strange worms never seen before. Vents are found along the mid-ocean ridges where the ocean floor is expanding.

Inventor's words

deep-sea
epibenthic sled
manipulators
oceanographer
submarine
submersible

Make a bottle aquarium

You will need

large plastic jar
styrofoam block
metallic fish stickers or
metallic paper • thin wire
shells and pebbles
crepe paper or tissue paper
reflective cardboard
colored cardboard
craft glue
paints and brush

1 Cut the back off a plastic jar to form the aquarium tank. Now glue a large chunk of styrofoam at the base of the tank and another at the top of the opening.

2 Cut out lots of little fish shapes from brightly colored metallic cardboard. Cut nine strips of thin wire, and on each one, glue 10 fish.

3 Paint the styrofoam base a sandy color, and glue some shells and pebbles in place.

4 Push the fish-covered wires into the styrofoam plugs. Then add crepe paper weeds, gluing them to the top and bottom of the aquarium.

5 Close the back of the aquarium by gluing on a panel of reflective cardboard. Now glue strips of colored cardboard around the base and neck of the jar to conceal the styrofoam.

What Else Can Fuel a Submarine?

In 1908, Britain launched the first diesel-powered submarine. Diesel was more powerful, cheaper to operate, and gave off fewer deadly fumes than gasoline. These engines need air to operate, though, so, like gasoline-powered submarines, they could not stay submerged for long.

During World War I (1914–1918), German U-boats proved just how effective submarines could be. In 1914, U-9 sank three British cruisers in one hour.

But even U-boats had a weakness. They had to surface every few hours for air. This made them targets for enemy planes or ships.

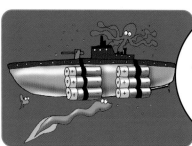

All early diesel-powered submarines had the same problem: when submerged for any length of time, they had to rely on electric battery power. In order to be truly under water, submarines needed a better power supply—but what?

We need the energy to stay under water for days at a time, or we'll be detected by the enemy.

WHAT HAPPENED NEXT?

- In 1945, for the first time, nuclear power was harnessed and used to destroy whole cities.

- But nuclear energy could also be put to good use. Scientists wanted to use it to create electricity supplies.

- They also believed it could be used to power certain vehicles. But because nuclear power was potentially dangerous, subs were stuck with gasoline and diesel engines.

- Then, in the United States, scientists suggested that nuclear energy could power ships, including submarines. Since nuclear power doesn't need air, that was good news.

We'll build a submarine that's powered by a small nuclear reactor that uses pressurized water and uranium fuel rods. The heat from the reactor will create steam, which will turn a turbine that will turn the propellers.

USS Nautilus was the first nuclear submarine. It was launched in 1954.

Nuclear fission

A **nuclear submarine** is a submarine that is powered by a **pressurized water reactor**, or **PWR**, a nuclear reactor that uses atomic **fission** to create energy. Atomic fission happens when **atoms** are split apart. Heated water from the reactor is passed along pipes to a steam **turbine**. Here, steam is created, causing the large turbine wheels to spin. The power from the turbine wheels rotates the propeller shaft and turns the propellers. The shaft is also connected to an electric motor that produces electricity for the submarine. The nuclear engine operates without air and uses far less fuel than other engines.

Steam heat

A pressurized water reactor, or PWR, is an engine that uses uranium fuel and water under high pressure to create energy.

Water is pressurized, or squeezed, in a pressurizer before it is pumped into the reactor core, or center, of the PWR. Inside the core are uranium fuel rods and control rods. As the water is pumped through, the nuclei of atoms in the uranium are made to split apart and release nuclear energy in the form of heat. This heats the water up to nearly 572 F (300 C). But because it is pressurized, it doesn't boil away. The hot pressurized water is then pumped into a heat exchanger, where it heats up ordinary water and turns it into steam. The steam is used to turn the submarine's turbines, which then turn its propeller. In condensers, the steam is cooled and returned to the heat exchanger.

Navigation is calculated and plotted in the control room of a nuclear submarine using GPS—Global Positioning System.

RECORD BREAKER

On its very first voyage, the nuclear submarine *Nautilus* proved that atomic energy was the best way to power a submarine. It broke every previous record for underwater speed and endurance. In 1958, it became the first submarine to sail under the ice cap at the North Pole.

Inventor's words

atom
condenser • core
nuclear submarine
fission
PWR
pressurized
turbine

Make a bottle sub

You will need

- large plastic bottle
- large and small yogurt containers
- thick cardboard
- craft knife • craft glue
- black marker
- skewer stick
- bendable drinking straw
- empty spool of thread
- paints and brush

1 Cut the bottle down the middle to one side of the lid. Cut the large container in half and glue onto the bottle end. Then cut a large oval window into the body of the sub.

2 Draw around the sub on a piece of cardboard. Cut out and design the interior. Split it into two decks and use pieces of cardboard to build walls between cabins.

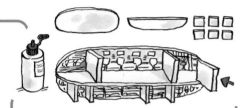

3 Paint and decorate the cabins. Make sure there's a bridge, torpedo room, engine room, and crew cabin.

4 For the conning tower, cut the small container in half, and cut a hole into the middle. Draw around it on some cardboard, cut out, and then design and color the inside with a ladder.

5 Paint the outer shell, and glue it over the interior (you may need to trim the deck and walls to fit). Add a cardboard and skewer stick propeller, a straw and thread spool periscope, and a cardboard nose fin.

How Can We Examine Wrecks?

Submersibles are used for many underwater activities, including exploration, mapping and repair, and building work. But sometimes it's too deep or dangerous for divers to stay submerged for as long as a job takes. But submersibles can't drive by themselves—can they?

Divers use submersibles for ordinary jobs such as looking for new marine life or fixing a damaged oil platform in cruel seas.

But some scientists would like to use submersibles to find ships that were sunk years ago, either by accident or through damage caused by enemy warships.

Until the invention of the submersible, no one dared dream that the Titanic or other great shipwrecks could be found. Looking for these wrecks posed difficulties that normal submersibles were unable to cope with.

Wouldn't it be great if we could investigate famous shipwrecks?

WHAT HAPPENED NEXT?

- Looking for a wreck can take years. Submersibles would have to be raised and lowered many times.

- A small submersible that would move quickly and into difficult underwater terrain was needed. But it might not be suitable for holding a diver.

- What if an unmanned submersible were used? It wouldn't pose any danger, and it could stay down for a long time.

- Good idea. But how can you control an unmanned vehicle at such a distance? Engineers worked on craft that were tethered, or tied, to a ship.

We'll design an advanced tethered vehicle (ATV). It'll be controlled by joysticks and will descend as a tether is unreeled from the ship. Sonar images from the ATV will appear on a screen in front of the operator.

ATVs are used by scientists to find sunken ships like the *Titanic*.

Sonar images

An **advanced tethered vehicle**, or **ATV**, is an unmanned submersible. It is operated from a special room on the deck of the mother ship. It is **tethered,** or tied, to the ship by control cables that unwind from a reel, like a fishing reel, as it descends. The ATV is operated by **joysticks**. Controlling the **thrusters**, or jets of air, can send the ATV in any direction. Joysticks also control video and still cameras that are mounted on the vehicle. A **sonar**, or sound wave, transmitter sends signals to the operator that are seen as images on a screen. The images show the shape of an object, even if there is little light available.

ATVs

In 1998, explorer Robert D. Ballard traveled to the Pacific Ocean to hunt for the *Yorktown*, an American aircraft carrier that had been sunk during World War II. He used an ATV.

When his ship was in the right position, he ordered the ATV to be lowered. It descended to 5,033 ft (1,534 m). Then, disaster! The tether cracked and water fused the electric line. After 24 hours, the ATV was fixed and ready to dive again. She reached 15,692 ft (4,783 m). But disaster struck again. Two glass instrument panels imploded with such force that cameras and computers were damaged. More repairs were needed. Finally, after yet another breakdown, the ATV reached the seabed at 16,599 ft (5,059 m). The sonar started pinging at an impact crater, and then the image of a flight deck could be seen. The ATV moved closer and, with lights and cameras working, perfectly relayed the first pictures of the *Yorktown* to Ballard.

GIANT WRECK

Robert D. Ballard also found the wreck of the *Titanic*. His work with the ATV showed that the hull of the great ship had not been ripped open by an iceberg, as had been assumed. Instead, the metal used to build the ship had become brittle with the cold. When the iceberg hit, it caused the hull to crack in some places—enough to sink the liner.

Ballard's ATV at work, exploring the wreckage of the *Yorktown*, in 1998

Inventor's words

ATV
joystick
sonar
tether
thruster

Model the *Titanic*

You will need

thick black cardboard
colored and white cardboard
thin cardboard tube
toothpicks
cotton thread or thin string
colored paper
craft glue • pencil
black marker
paint and brush

1 Cut two long lengths of thick black cardboard. Tape at both ends. Now cut two short panels the same height as the long pieces. Glue them in place across the width, so the hull of the ship bulges in the middle.

2 Draw around the shape of the hull on some colored cardboard to make the deck shape. Glue into place. Cut away the bow and stern shapes from the body.

3 Draw and cut out a simple super structure from white cardboard, making sure to leave a flap at the bottom with which to tape it to the deck. Use a black marker to draw in the tiny windows.

4 Cut a thin cardboard tube into four pieces to make funnels. Paint the funnels and superstructure before gluing all the parts together.

5 Decorate further by adding toothpick masts, cotton rigging, paper flags, and bunting.

Can People Live in the Sea?

Scientists and underwater explorers have found many ways for divers to explore the ocean. They can use diving suits connected to a ship, scuba equipment, or a submersible. But deep-sea diving can be dangerous—in most cases, divers need to decompress when returning to the surface.

Decompression means returning to the surface very slowly in order to avoid "the bends"—when air bubbles form in the blood. This can be fatal.

Sometimes decompression chambers are used to help eliminate the nitrogen through normal breathing. Even so, divers can't stay down too long or too deep.

We need to spend much more time under the sea to explore it properly.

This means no one can actually live under the sea for any length of time. But scientists know that much more exploration could take place, if only divers could stay below longer.

WHAT HAPPENED NEXT?

- The invention of the bathyscaphe and bathysphere allowed divers to stay down for longer periods of time. But even these craft had to surface after a while.

- It was also difficult for divers to go in and out of the craft while it was submerged.

- Jacques Cousteau had already developed the aqualung to help divers operate with more freedom. He now turned to finding ways to allow divers to stay below for longer.

- What was needed was an undersea living station. But how could scientists solve the problem of water pressure?

We'll need to erect buildings on the seafloor. They can be built up to 594 ft (180 m) beneath the surface. Compressed breathing gas will be kept in special compartments. Divers will be able to live and work there for many weeks.

Scientists work under the sea in this saturation habitat.

A long stay

A **saturation habitat** is a manned station built under the surface of the sea. Usually, it consists of one or more buildings erected on the seabed. Inside the buildings are special compartments that are filled with **compressed** breathing gas. This allows the scientists and technicians working in the habitat to breathe at the same pressure as that outside the habitat. The pressure in the buildings is regulated. Divers don't need to **decompress** as they would if they were returning to the surface. Saturation habitats allow divers to stay under water for many weeks at a time.

Decompression

Saturation diving is used when work has to be done at great depths under the ocean. The diver is pressurized, or squeezed by the surrounding air, in a pressure chamber on board the sub. The pressure is the same as the pressure under water. When the diver finishes work, returning to a decompression chamber will reduce the surrounding air pressure.

Although the air around us presses on our bodies, we don't notice it. Like air, water also presses on the bodies of divers. The deeper they go, the more pressure there is. The pressure may become great enough to squeeze the air completely out of a diver's body. So, the air the diver breathes is compressed to compensate. If the diver returns to the surface too quickly, air inside the body may expand, causing bubbles to form in the blood. This is called the bends. To prevent this, decompression chambers are used to reduce the pressure slowly.

DANGER

Oil rigs at sea constantly need checking and repairing. This is often done by submersibles. But sometimes these machines do not have the right tools for the job. This means a diver has to do it. Repairing oil rigs is a dangerous job. Divers have to be skilled and brave, as seas can be rough and unpredictable.

Divers decompress in a special chamber.

Inventor's words

bends • compress
decompress
decompression
chamber
pressurized
saturation diving
saturation habitat
submersible

Make a bubble dome

You will need

styrofoam cups and bowls
plastic drink bottles
small plastic salad bowl
thick cardboard • pencil
craft glue
double-sided tape
plastic lid • bottle caps
bendable drinking straws
small pebbles • glitter glue

1 To make a tower, cut the top off a styrofoam cup. Glue a cardboard circle to the open end and a bottle cap on top of that. Now glue three straws to the bottom. Paint on tiny windows and glitter glue details. Repeat to make two towers.

2 Follow the same process to make the main building, this time using a larger styrofoam bowl. The drinking straw legs can be bent into a horizontal position.

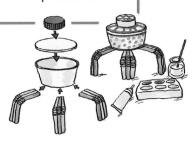

3 Make a platform by cutting out a large piece of cardboard that your city will sit on. Now cut out similar pieces, each one slightly larger than the previous one. Glue one on top of the other, and glue on small stones before painting.

4 Cut the top off two plastic bottles, and cover the towers with them. Cover the main building with a plastic bowl. Glue to attach.

5 Cut another bottle in half lengthwise, and make connecting tunnels from the towers to the main building.

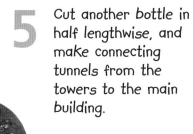

Glossary

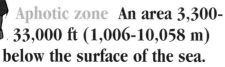

Aphotic zone An area 3,300-33,000 ft (1,006-10,058 m) below the surface of the sea. There is no light at all at this depth.

Aqualung A portable underwater breathing apparatus. It allows a diver to breathe under water.

Atom A tiny part of an element, or simple substance, made up of an electron or electrons that move around a nucleus. The nucleus is made up of neutrons and protons. All the atoms in an element are the same.

ATV Stands for advanced tethered vehicle, a kind of unmanned submersible.

Ballast Heavy material placed in the hold of a ship or submarine to give it stability or to add weight.

Barbel A kind of fin found in front of some deep-sea fish's mouths. It is used to lure smaller fish into the larger fish's mouth.

Barotrauma An injury that happens if the pressure of the water around divers is too great compared to the air pressure in their lungs. It is also called squeeze.

Bathyscaphe A manned vessel used for deep-sea exploration.

Bathysphere A ball-shaped container that can be hung underneath a ship or lowered to a depth of about 2,970 ft (900 m) below the surface.

Bends When a diver ascends from the deep too fast, bubbles of nitrogen gas form in the blood. They can then block the flow of blood and kill the diver. This is called the bends.

Buoyancy The ability of something to stay afloat.

Buoyancy compensator A device that can be inflated by a scuba diver to help maintain a required depth.

Compressed Squeezed into a smaller space.

Condenser In a pressurized water reactor, a device in which steam is cooled and returned to the heat exchanger.

Core The center of a PWR. It contains fuel rods and control rods.

Decompress To lessen the pressure on a diver caused by the water around them. Decompression happens when a diver returns to the surface.

Decompression chamber A special chamber that slowly reduces the air pressure around a diver when he or she returns to the surface from deep under water.

Deep-sea Parts of the oceans that are pitch black and where the huge pressure from the surrounding water would crush any land-living animal.

Deep-sea fish Fish that live in the deep sea.

Demand valve A device connected by hose to air tanks and held in a diver's mouth, also called a demand regulator. When the diver breathes in, the valve supplies air.

Depth The measurement from the surface of the water downward.

Disphotic zone An area from 660-3,300 ft (200-1,000 m) below the surface of the ocean. It is often called the twilight zone, as there is very little light to be seen there.

Diving plane A kind of wing attached to a submarine. They are tilted to help the craft descend.

Diving suit A waterproof suit and helmet that is supplied with air from the surface.

Epibenthic sled A kind of scoop used to scoop up material from the deep sea. It gave scientists their first glimpse of life as it existed at this depth.

Fiberglass A strong and lightweight material made by mixing fibers of glass with a sticky, liquid resin, which then hardens.

Fission How something is broken into two or more parts. Atomic fission happens when atoms split apart.

Gasoline A liquid made from petroleum. The process involves fractional distillation and cracking. Gasoline is used as a fuel.

Hull The body of a any ship, submersible, or submarine.

Joystick A kind of steering mechanism used on an ATV. It is stick-shaped device that is secured at one end and can move backwards, forwards, and to the sides.

Limpet mine A kind of mine that can be attached to another object in the same way a limpet attaches itself to things.

Manipulators Mechanical arms that can pick up material from the seafloor, used on submersibles.

Nuclear submarine A submarine powered by a pressurized water reactor, a kind of nuclear reactor that uses atomic fission to create energy.

Oceanographer A scientist who studies the oceans.

Photic zone An area 0-660 ft (0-200 m) beneath the surface of the oceans. It receives enough light for algae to carry out the process of photosynthesis.

Photophore Organs inside a deep-sea fish's body that allow it to make its own light.

Port The small round windows in a bathysphere.

Pressurized Under pressure or being squeezed by a substance such as water or air.

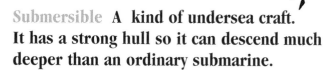

Propulsion The action of pushing or driving something forward.

PWR The abbreviation for pressurized water reactor, an engine that uses uranium fuel and water under high pressure to create energy.

Saturation diving Diving at great depths under the ocean. Divers are pressurized, or squeezed, by the air around them in a pressure chamber for the great pressure at depth.

Saturation habitat A manned station consisting of one or more buildings with special compressed air breathing compartments and built under the surface of the sea.

Scuba Scuba diving involves the use of tanks to supply air to a diver as well as other kinds of equipment. Scuba stands for self-contained underwater breathing apparatus.

Sonar The use of sound waves to transmit signals to an operator who sees the signals as images on a screen.

Streamlining Creating a smooth flowing shape. It is important to ships, submarines, and aircraft, as it helps them decrease turbulence.

Submarine A ship that can travel under water as well as on the surface. Many submarines are warships.

Submersible A kind of undersea craft. It has a strong hull so it can descend much deeper than an ordinary submarine.

Tether A rope or chain or some other device that holds an object.

Thrusters Jets of air that are used to propel some vehicles, including ATVs.

Turbine A power device that uses heated water passed along pipes to a turbine wheel, where steam is created that spins the large turbine. The power from the turbine wheels rotates and can power vehicles such as ships and submarines.

Turbulence A disturbance in water or air that happens when a vehicle moves through it. Streamlining avoids turbulence.

Water pressure The pressure on an object submerged in water caused by the water, so that the more water surrounding an object, the greater the pressure on it will be.

Wet suit Scuba divers wear a wet suit made of special material to keep them warm.

X-craft The original name given to the mini-submarines used by the British navy during World War II. Each craft carried four men.

Index

Tools and Materials

Almost all of the materials in this book can be found around the house or bought at your local art or craft shop. If you cannot find the exact item, try to replace it with something similar.

Most of the models will stick fast with craft glue or even wallpaper paste. However, some materials need a stronger glue, so be careful when using these, as they may damage your clothes and even your skin. Ask an adult to help you.

Always cover furniture with newspaper or a large cloth, and protect your clothes by wearing a work apron.

User Care

Take special care when handling sharp tools such as scissors, pointed gadgets, pieces of wire, or craft knives. Ask an adult to help you when you need to use them.